- Gorillas are the largest type of ape.

- A male gorilla can weigh up to 500 pounds!

- Like all apes, gorillas do not have tails.

- A group of gorillas living together is called a troop.

- Some troops have more than 50 members. Others have just two.

- Baby gorillas learn by watching their moms and other gorillas.

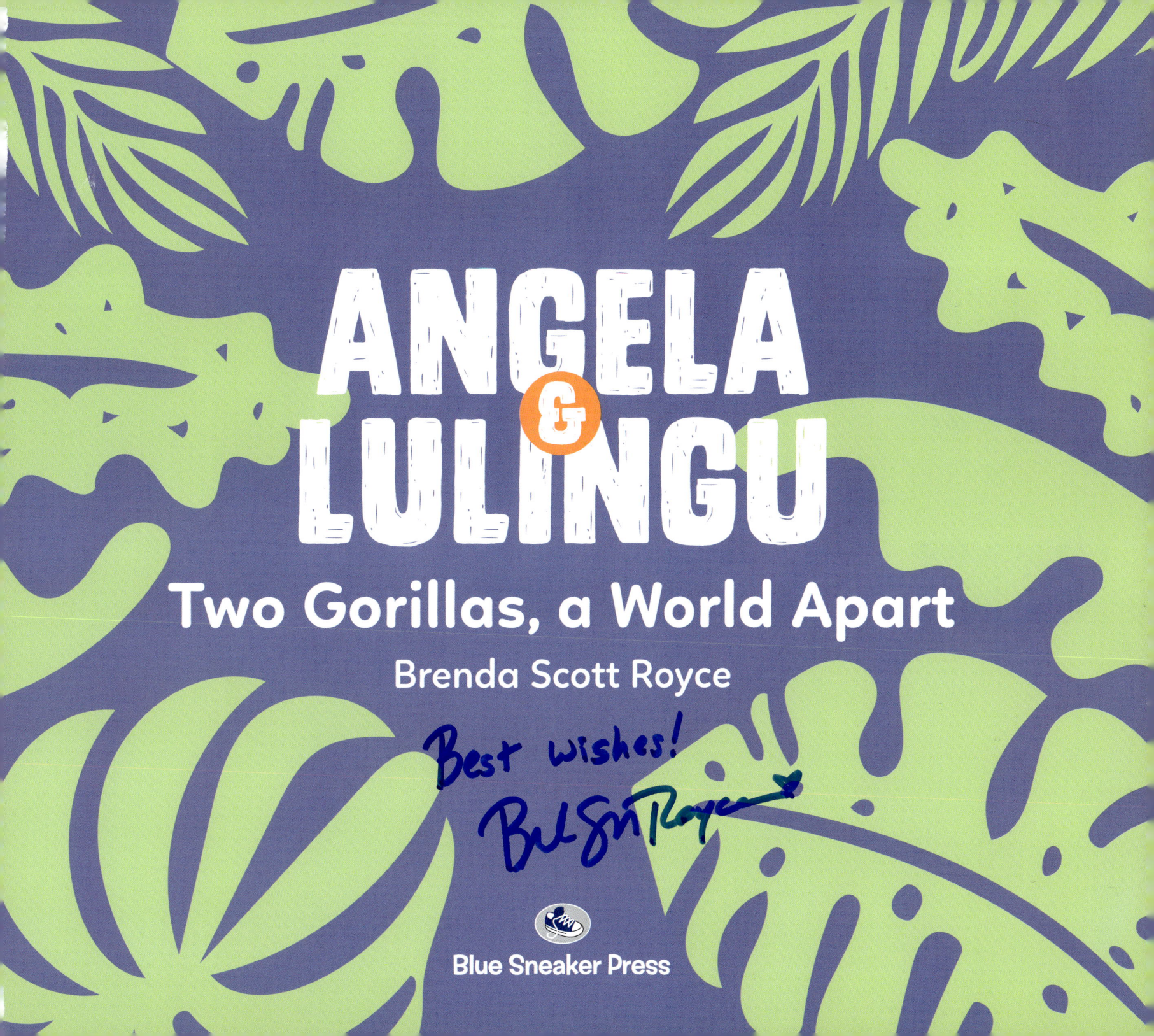

ANGELA & LULINGU

Two Gorillas, a World Apart

Brenda Scott Royce

Best wishes!
Brenda Scott Royce

Blue Sneaker Press

Angela & Lulingu: Two Gorillas, a World Apart was published by Blue Sneaker Press. Blue Sneaker works with authors, illustrators, nonprofit organizations, and corporations to publish books that engage, entertain, and educate children on subjects that affect our world.

Blue Sneaker Press is an imprint of Southwestern Publishing House, Inc., 2451 Atrium Way, Nashville, TN 37214.
Southwestern Publishing House is a wholly owned subsidiary of Southwestern Family of Companies, Nashville, Tennessee.

Christopher G. Capen, President, Southwestern Publishing House
Carrie Hasler, Publisher, Blue Sneaker Press
Kristin Connelly, Managing Editor
Mary Velgos, Senior Art Director
swpublishinghouse.com | 800-358-0560

Text copyright © 2023 Los Angeles Zoo and Botanical Gardens

All rights reserved. No part of this book may be reproduced or transmitted in any form or by any means, electronic or mechanical, including photocopying or recording, or by any information retrieval system, without the written permission of the copyright holder.

ISBN: 978-1-943198-19-1

Library of Congress Control Number: 2023901066

Printed in China

10 9 8 7 6 5 4 3 2 1

Blue Sneaker Press

Los Angeles Zoo

ACKNOWLEDGMENTS

This book would not have been possible without the support of the entire teams at the Los Angeles Zoo and Botanical Gardens, Greater Los Angeles Zoo Association, and Gorilla Rehabilitation and Conservation Education (GRACE) Center, with special thanks to the following individuals:

LOS ANGELES ZOO: Denise M. Verret, Beth Schaefer, Candace Sclimenti, Megan Fox, Tania Prebble, Dr. Jordan Davis-Powell, Dr. Jake Owens, Dan Keeffe, and Renae Cotero.

GREATER LOS ANGELES ZOO ASSOCIATION: Tom Jacobson, Kait Hilliard, Janet Dial, Rob Woolley, Genie Vasels, and Jamie Pham.

GRACE GORILLAS: Tommi Wolfe, Laurie Cummins, Dr. Katie Fawcett, Rory Keating, Jackson Kabuyaya Mbeke, Dalmas Kakule Syangeha, Jean Baptiste Kambale Muviri, Devotte Kavira Kirihi, and Aldegonde Kavuo Saambili.

Team Angela at the L.A. Zoo includes Megan Fox, Beth Schaefer, Denise M. Verret, Dr. Jordan Davis-Powell, Candace Sclimenti, and Tania Prebble.

This book idea originated as part of the author's graduate work through Miami University's Advanced Inquiry Program in conjunction with San Diego Zoo Wildlife Alliance. Special thanks to Dr. Mackenzie Borau, Marina Karastamatis, and Alicia Lamfers for their support and guidance, and to Georgeanne Irvine for paving the way and inspiring others to follow.

Lastly, special thanks to all involved in Lulingu's rescue and transport, including staff and volunteers with Gorilla Doctors, the Congolese Institute for the Conservation of Nature (ICCN), and the Senkwekwe Centre at Virunga National Park.

DEDICATION

This book is dedicated to Betty White. Betty's love of animals was legendary, and she had a soft spot for gorillas. Her passion for the L.A. Zoo and its mission inspired thousands of people to donate in her memory. This book grew out of that loving legacy.

IMAGE CREDITS: Jamie Pham/©Los Angeles Zoo: front cover left, copyright page top, acknowledgments, 4, 6, 7, 8, 9, 10, 11, 12, 13, 14 upper, 15, 22 lower, 28 lower right, 29 upper left and center, 30 lower left, 31 upper left, 32 upper left and right, 33 upper left, 34 second and fourth from top, 35 (all except center left), 36 upper right. ©GRACE Gorillas: front cover right, copyright page bottom, 5, 16 upper, 17 lower left and right, 22 upper, 24 right, 25 upper, 26 lower, 28 left and upper right, 29 upper right, 30 upper and lower right, 31 lower right, 32 lower left, 33 lower left, 36 left. Shutterstock/stopkin: front and back endsheet vector design. Shutterstock/Igillustrator: front and back endsheet vector design. GoPro/©GRACE Gorillas: 16 lower, 17 upper, 19, 20, 21, 23 upper, 25 lower left foreground and lower right, 27 lower right, 33 right. ©Andrew Bernard: 23 lower, 25 lower left foreground, 27 upper right, 34 third from top. Tania Prebble: 29 lower, 31 upper right. ©Adam Kiefer: 18 upper and lower right. ©Liz Williamson: 26 upper, 27 upper left. ©Deni Béchard: back cover, 24 left. Tad Motoyama/©Los Angeles Zoo: 14 lower left. Max Block: 14 lower right. ©Virunga National Park: 18 lower left. LouAnne Brickhouse: 36 lower right. Professorsolo2015, CC BY-SA 4.0, via Wikimedia Commons: 19 lower right. Shutterstock/Kit Korzun: 34 upper left. Shutterstock/flickr4466: 35 center left.

ANGELA AND LULINGU

Angela and Lulingu (lew-LING-goo) are two young gorillas that live on opposite sides of the world. Angela lives with her family at the Los Angeles Zoo in California, and Lulingu lives at GRACE, a **wildlife sanctuary** in the Democratic Republic of the Congo (DRC) in the heart of Africa.

Angela and Lulingu live

LOS ANGELES

The Los Angeles Zoo is dedicated to saving wildlife, enriching communities, and creating connections to nature.

Angela is a western lowland gorilla.

words to know
A **wildlife sanctuary** is a place that provides animals with shelter and safety.

more than 9,000 miles apart!

DEMOCRATIC REPUBLIC OF THE CONGO

GRACE stands for Gorilla Rehabilitation and Conservation Education.

They live on separate continents and have different stories, but both gorillas have very important jobs. Angela and Lulingu inspire others to care about gorilla **species** all around the world.

Lulingu is a Grauer's gorilla.

words to know
A **species** is a group of related animals.

ANGELA'S STORY

On a bright January morning in Los Angeles, a mother gorilla named N'djia (en-JEE-uh) cuddles her newborn baby. Cradling the infant in one arm, N'djia leans forward and presses her lips to the top of the baby's head. Zookeeper Tania watches in amazement, wiping happy tears from her eyes.

The Animal Care Team quietly observed N'djia's first moments with her newborn.

ANGELA'S STORY

N'djia was a caring mom right from the start.

It's an exciting day at the Los Angeles Zoo. The baby girl is the first gorilla born at the Zoo in more than 20 years. Her birth is big news. Her photo will appear in newspapers and magazines. Crowds of people will come to see her. But for now, N'djia and her baby are enjoying some quiet time together behind the scenes at the Zoo's gorilla habitat, Campo Gorilla Reserve.

MEET MOM!

N'djia was named after a village in Cameroon, an African country that is home to wild gorillas. Born at the San Diego Zoo Safari Park in 1994, N'djia moved to the Los Angeles Zoo in 2018.

Getting Ready

Throughout the day, other members of the Zoo's Animal Care Team come to get a glimpse of the baby. They had been preparing for this day for months—ever since they learned N'djia was pregnant. They coached her to sit still for **ultrasound** exams, so they could see if the baby was developing normally.

words to know

An **ultrasound** uses sound waves to create a picture of what's going on inside the body of a human or animal.

It can be hard to tell if a gorilla is pregnant. Gorillas' bellies are naturally big due to their bulky diet.

ANGELA'S STORY

N'djia was taught to bring a plushie to her keepers.

The team also needed to make sure N'djia would be ready to be a mother. The gorilla had never had a baby before. Would she know what to do?

N'djia's keepers had taught her to retrieve different objects, including a gorilla plushie. N'djia quickly learned to pick up the requested item and bring it to her keepers. It was a fun game with a serious purpose. They had to be sure that if N'djia's baby ever became sick or injured, she would bring it to them.

An animal caregiver gives N'djia an ultrasound.

The baby gorilla weighed about four pounds at birth.

Welcome, Baby!

When the time came for N'djia to give birth, everything went smoothly. Dr. Jordan Davis-Powell, one of the Zoo's veterinarians, was first to examine the newborn. She was pleased to see the baby holding up her tiny head and clinging tightly to N'djia. The baby's bright eyes and loud cries were also good signs. The baby was healthy, strong, and absolutely adorable. The doctor announced, "Mom and baby are doing great!"

Dr. Jordan Davis-Powell

ANGELA'S STORY

MOM-IN-TRAINING

Gorillas learn by observing others. At the San Diego Zoo, N'djia had been around gorilla moms and babies. When her time came, she knew just how to take care of her own daughter.

"We are watching them very closely," said zookeeper Tania. "Is the baby alert? Is mom holding her properly? Is she nursing?" One by one, the keepers checked all the boxes. "We are all so very happy."

The next day, N'djia brought her baby outside into the gorilla habitat for the first time. Zoo visitors were thrilled to get a glimpse of the little one.

The baby gorilla was named Angela after Angela Collier, a generous person who devoted her life to helping animals and the places that take care of them.

Banana plants are grown at the L.A. Zoo as food for the gorillas.

VEGGIE LOVERS!

Gorillas are herbivores. They mostly eat leaves, bark, and stems. Their diet also includes fruits, seeds, and even some insects.

ANGELA'S STORY

Angela's caretakers took notes on her growth and celebrated every milestone. She was one month old when her first tooth appeared. (Human babies get their first tooth at about six months of age.) Though she was still nursing from her mother, Angela began testing out other foods. Tomatoes and carrots became Angela's favorite treats. Soon, Angela was strong enough to ride on N'djia's back. Sometimes, Angela would climb on top of her mother's head!

Introducing the Family

Angela gets a lot of attention from the other members of her family. Dad Kelly is very protective. He keeps a watchful eye on his daughter. The silverback of the family group, Kelly is known for his peaceful personality. Being a silverback is serious business—but sometimes Kelly can't resist Angela's invitations to play.

When the grown-ups aren't in the mood to play, Angela entertains herself. She enjoys tumbling head over heels down the hillside.

Dad Kelly

ANGELA'S STORY

Evelyn

Rapunzel

Like humans, gorillas are very social animals. The bonds they form can last a lifetime.

Rapunzel is like Angela's "auntie." From day one, Rapunzel was eager to hold the new baby. She soon began carrying Angela around the habitat whenever she could.

The Zoo's oldest gorilla, Evelyn, was slower to form a bond with Angela. For several months, Evelyn kept her distance. Finally, one day, Zoo visitors saw the two playing and cuddling. Friends at last!

LEADER OF THE TROOP

Adult male gorillas are called silverbacks because of the silvery-white hair on their backs. A group of gorillas living together, called a troop, typically has just one silverback, along with females and their young.

LULINGU'S STORY

Like Angela, Lulingu is the youngest member of her troop. She lives at GRACE, a sanctuary in the Democratic Republic of the Congo, Africa.

Situated high on a mountaintop and surrounded by miles and miles of forest, GRACE is a green oasis—a peaceful place in a country with many challenges.

GRACE is currently home to 14 rescued gorillas.

GRACE Gorilla Sanctuary

LULINGU'S STORY

Lulingu spends most of her day exploring protected forest habitat with other members of her group. They search for wild fruits, rest in tall grass, and race each other to the tops of trees. By nightfall, they return to the sanctuary. They are welcomed by their caregivers, men and women who have devoted their lives to protecting gorillas.

GRACE'S YOUNGEST

Lulingu is a Grauer's gorilla. GRACE is the world's only sanctuary for this type of gorilla. Lulingu was the youngest gorilla ever to arrive at GRACE.

GRACE's team of caregivers

A Challenging Start

Lulingu's life was not always so peaceful. Born in the wild, she lived with her family for less than a year when tragedy struck. **Poachers** killed her mother... and took Lulingu away from the forest.

Luckily for Lulingu, people heard about her capture and wanted to help. Many kindhearted people—including park rangers, community leaders, and veterinarians—worked together to arrange for her rescue and transfer to GRACE.

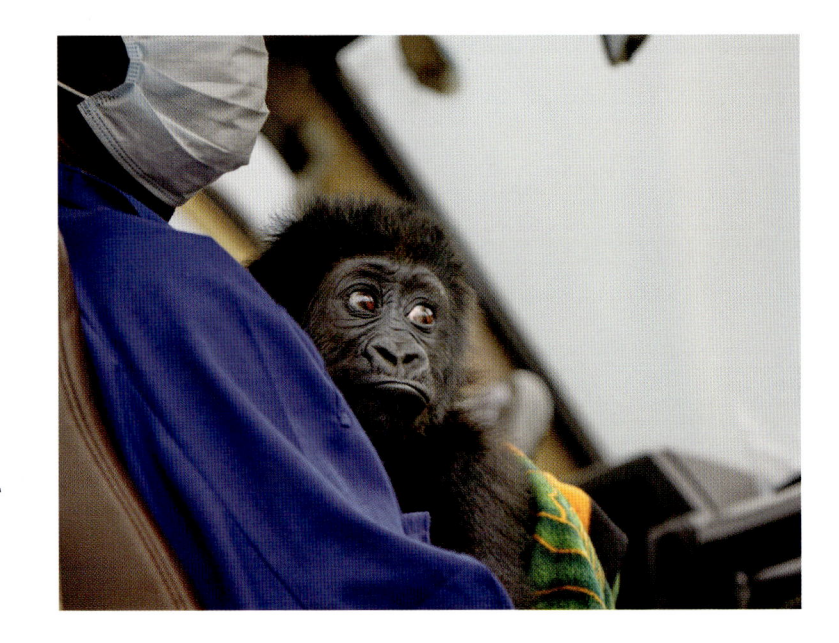

words to know

Poaching is the illegal hunting of wild animals, including apes.

Pilot Anthony Caere was one of several people who helped Lulingu travel safely to GRACE.

NAMING LULINGU

Lulingu was named after the village where she was rescued.

Lulingu was injured from being kept in chains, and she was very hungry. Otherwise, she was healthy. Once she was strong enough, she began the long journey to GRACE. Lulingu and her helpers traveled by car, ferry, and even airplane. The young ape was curious during the trip, often looking out the window at the world passing by. Finally, after a trip of nearly two days, she reached her new home.

LULINGU'S STORY

At first, Lulingu was cared for at Senkwekwe Centre, a mountain gorilla orphanage. To ease her transition to GRACE, one of Lulingu's new caregivers, Aldegonde, traveled with Lulingu.

Caring for Lulingu

Gorilla babies stick close to their mothers for the first three years of life. But Lulingu had lost her mother. So, the team at GRACE cared for Lulingu as a mother would: carrying, feeding, and playing with her. Most importantly, they made sure she felt safe and loved.

Caregiver Kambale

Caregiver Devotte carries Lulingu on her back like a gorilla mother would.

LULINGU'S STORY

Caregivers Kambale and Devotte took turns caring for Lulingu. Day or night, the little gorilla was never alone. When Lulingu was scared or angry, they held her close and made soft, grunting sounds like a gorilla. At first, Lulingu drank milk from a baby bottle. Gradually, her caregivers got her to try solid foods like passion fruit and plums.

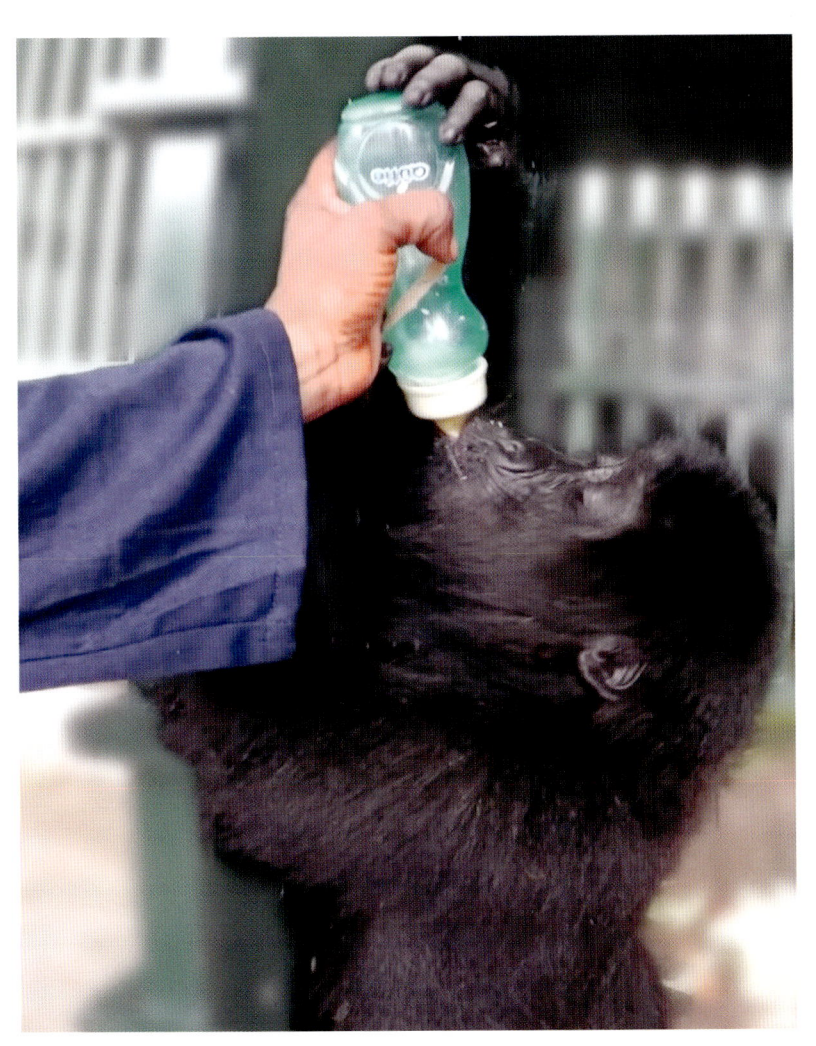

Kambale and Devotte brought Lulingu to the forest to practice climbing trees. Kambale climbed first so that Lulingu would follow. Her caregivers taught her how to find and eat wild foods. Her favorites include wild bananas and elephant grass.

It takes very special people to nurse gorilla **orphans** back to health and help them cope with the loss of their families. As much as Kambale and Devotte loved taking care of Lulingu, they knew she belonged with the other gorillas.

words to know

An **orphan** is a person or animal who has lost its parents.

GENTLE GIANTS

Often called "gentle giants," gorillas are known for their peaceful personalities. But they are super strong and will use their strength to defend themselves if they feel threatened. So, gorilla introductions must be managed very carefully.

LULINGU'S STORY

Lulingu was eager to meet the other gorillas. She knew they were nearby. She could hear them, smell them, and sometimes see them.

After a few months of round-the-clock care, it was time for Lulingu to join the other gorillas. She had grown strong and confident. She was ready.

Devotte brings Lulingu to meet the rest of the gorillas through a protective gate.

A New Family for Lulingu

At long last, Lulingu's **integration** day arrived! The staff decided that Lulingu should meet Pinga first. As the troop's alpha, or dominant, female, Pinga was the boss. If she liked Lulingu, the others would follow. But if Pinga didn't like Lulingu, things could be tough for the little one.

MEET PINGA!

A born leader with a sweet side, Pinga is one of GRACE's oldest—and largest—gorillas. She had previously adopted other orphans as her own babies. The staff hoped she would do the same with Lulingu.

words to know

Integration is when different groups or individuals form one group together.

LULINGU'S STORY

The other gorillas remained outside in the yard. Inside, Pinga and Lulingu waited in separate rooms. The GRACE staff held their breaths as they opened the gate that separated the two gorillas. Would Pinga accept Lulingu into the troop—or would she reject the newcomer?

Pinga and Lulingu waited on opposite sides of a gate until it was time to meet.

Pinga rushed toward Lulingu and scooped the young gorilla into her arms. She held her close. Everyone cheered!

Soon, it was time for Lulingu to meet the rest of her new family. The pair went outside, Pinga carrying Lulingu on her back like a proud mother. She protected Lulingu when the older gorillas got a little rough. They were curious about the youngster!

LULINGU'S STORY

Shamavu

Jackson, GRACE's DRC director, was thrilled to see Lulingu become part of the gorilla family.

Lulingu quickly got to know the other members of her troop. One of her closest friends is Shamavu, a playful male gorilla. They enjoy climbing, laughing, and wrestling.

Kambale and Devotte miss cuddling and caring for Lulingu, but they are happy to see her once again living among gorillas. The gorillas at GRACE share a history of heartbreak. They are all orphans. But they helped each other heal, forming a tight-knit family.

A DAY IN THE LIFE OF ANGELA AND LULINGU

Angela and Lulingu live in different places and have different stories, but they also have a lot in common.

Both are loved by their gorilla families—and their human caregivers. Lulingu was adopted by Pinga at a sanctuary. Angela was raised by her mother, N'djia, at a zoo.

Lulingu and Pinga

Lulingu spends time in the trees.

Angela and N'djia

Angela

ANGELA AND LULINGU

BIRTHDAY TREAT

Zookeepers celebrate Angela's birthday on January 18 with a "cake" made out of fruits and cereal. Lulingu's birth date is unknown. Her rescuers estimated her age based on her size and teeth.

The gorillas at the Los Angeles Zoo spend their days outside in their habitat. At the end of the day, keepers use a sound-maker to call the gorillas inside for their supper. *Clack, clack, clack.*

At GRACE, the gorillas explore the forest throughout the day. The sound of a triangle tells them it's time to return to their night house. *Clang, clang, clang.*

Caregivers at GRACE grow and prepare fresh food for the gorillas.

Both gorillas get check-ups to make sure they remain healthy. They've been trained to allow staff to take their temperature and give them medicine or vaccines when needed.

Accredited zoos and sanctuaries, like the Los Angeles Zoo and GRACE, must meet high standards for animal care.

ANGELA AND LULINGU

The night buildings at GRACE and the L.A. Zoo have multiple rooms. Gorillas have their choice of where to go and whom to hang out with.

Gorillas build night nests to sleep in. Infants share a nest with their mothers. Now that Lulingu and Angela are getting older, they both sometimes want to sleep on their own.

SUPERSTARS!

From the day she was born, Angela has been a social media sensation. People travel from all over the world to see her at the Los Angeles Zoo.

BUILDING CONNECTIONS

In 2022, the L.A. Zoo and GRACE teamed up to connect two classrooms—one in Los Angeles and the other in Kasugho, DRC. The kids in each place learned about gorillas: where they live, what they eat, and how they spend their days. The students heard Angela's and Lulingu's stories and pledged to be "Gorilla Heroes," helping to spread the word about these awesome animals.

words to know

An animal is an **ambassador** for its species when it inspires people to care not just about that individual, but also about its relatives all over the world.

ANGELA AND LULINGU

A video of Lulingu playing and laughing went viral in 2017. The video has been viewed by millions of people. Laughter isn't just for humans. Gorillas laugh, too. Lulingu's laugh sounds like a breathy "hee-hee-hee."

These gorillas have fans around the world. People who may never be able to travel to Los Angeles or Africa have gotten to know them—and love them. These amazing **ambassadors** inspire others to care about gorillas and learn more about them.

GORILLA SPECIES

There are two gorilla species, or types. Each species is divided into two subspecies, or categories.

WESTERN GORILLA
- Cross River gorilla
- Western lowland gorilla

EASTERN GORILLA
- Grauer's gorilla
- Mountain gorilla

Cross River Gorilla

Western Lowland Gorilla

Grauer's Gorilla

Mountain Gorilla

All gorillas are endangered. Threats to their survival include:
- Poaching.
- Wildlife trafficking—some babies are taken to be sold as pets.
- Habitat loss—trees are being cut down for logging, for living space, and for mining metals and ores.

DID YOU KNOW?

Baby gorillas have white patches of hair on their rumps. These tail tufts disappear by about three or four years of age.

Gorillas, especially adult males, beat their chests to communicate their size and strength. The sound can travel a long way through the forest.

Gorillas walk on all fours with their fingers curled under. This is called knuckle-walking.

RECYCLE!

Coltan is a rare ore that is used in cell phones. Recycling old electronics helps gorillas by reducing the need for mining in gorilla habitat.

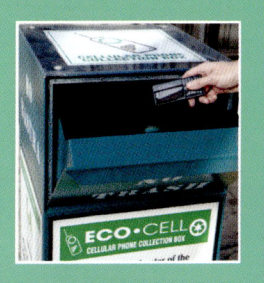

Like humans, gorillas have **opposable** thumbs. But unlike ours, their big toes are opposable, too! Flexible toes help gorillas climb trees and hold food.

words to know

An **opposable** thumb can rotate and touch the other fingers of the same hand.

PROUD PARTNERS

No one person or organization can save a species. It takes teamwork!

GRACE works with local communities to make forests safer for gorillas. Team members teach their neighbors to live in harmony with wildlife. The community takes great pride in their gorillas. GRACE plans to one day release gorillas from the sanctuary back into the wild. The hope is that every orphan rescued will be the last.

L.A. Zoo Chief Veterinarian Dr. Dominique Keller examines a hornbill.

The Los Angeles Zoo supports **conservation** organizations around the world, including GRACE. The Zoo provides expert advice and training to gorilla caregivers. It also donates money to develop education programs and maintain facilities and roads.

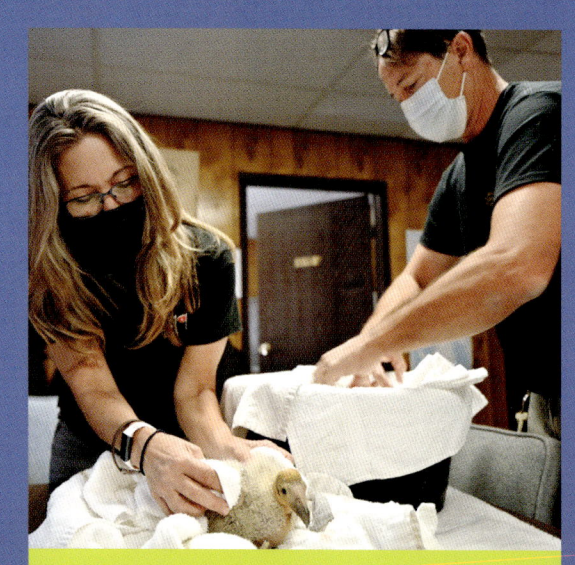

Local students learn about gorillas at GRACE.

The Los Angeles Zoo works with its partners to protect gorillas and other endangered species. Healthy, thriving zoo populations ensure that they will never, ever disappear from the planet.

words to know

Conservation is the act of protecting wildlife or nature.

Zookeepers care for a critically endangered California condor chick.

YOU CAN HELP!

- The Los Angeles Zoo and GRACE Gorillas are working together to build a brighter future for gorillas. And you can help!

- Learn more about gorillas and other endangered animals by visiting the websites for the L.A. Zoo and GRACE Gorillas:

  www.lazoo.org   www.gracegorillas.org

- Create a poster or video to teach others about gorillas.

- Recycle your old electronics—this will reduce the need for mining in gorilla habitat. Many zoos, including the L.A. Zoo, have collection bins. The money raised is donated to gorilla conservation programs.

Watch videos of Lulingu's rescue and Angela playing,
and download free gorilla activities at:

www.lazoo.org/TwoGorillas

- Playing helps young gorillas learn new skills.

- Playing also helps gorillas make friends.

- Gorillas usually live to be 35 to 40 years old.

- No two gorilla noses are alike.

- Each gorilla has its own noseprint—the pattern of wrinkles and indentations around its nose.

- Gorillas have 10 fingers and 10 toes, just like humans.